It's fun to draw Knights and Castles

Mark Bergin

SKY PONY PRESS
NEW YORK

Mark Bergin was born in Hastings, England. He has illustrated an award-winning series and written over twenty books. He has done many book designs, layouts, and storyboards in many styles including cartoon for numerous books, posters, and advertisements. He lives in Bexhill-on-sea with his wife and three children.

HOW TO USE THIS BOOK:

Start by following the numbered splats on the left-hand page. These steps will ask you to add some lines to your drawing. The new lines are always drawn in red so you can see how the drawing builds from step to step. Read the "You can do it!" splats to learn about drawing and coloring techniques you can use.

Sky Pony Press books may be purchased in bulk at special discounts for sales promotion, corporate gifts, fund-raising, or educational purposes. Special editions can also be created to specifications. For details, contact the Special Sales Department, Sky Pony Press, 307 West 36th Street, 11th Floor, New York, NY 10018 or info@skyhorsepublishing.com.

Sky Pony® is a registered trademark of Skyhorse Publishing, Inc.®, a Delaware corporation.

Visit our website at www.skyponypress.com.

10 9 8 7 6 5 4 3 2 1

Manufactured in China, October 2012
This product conforms to CPSIA 2008

Library of Congress Cataloging-in-Publication Data

Bergin, Mark, 1961-
It's fun to draw knights and castles / Mark Bergin.
pages cm
Includes index.
ISBN 978-1-62087-113-3 (pbk. : alk. paper) 1. Knights and knighthood in art--Juvenile literature. 2. Castles in art--Juvenile literature. 3. Drawing--Technique--Juvenile literature. I. Title.
NC825.K54B473 2013
743'.8--dc23
2012038263

Contents

Castle guard

1 Start with the helmet. Add eye slots and dots for breathing holes.

2 Add a shield. Draw in markings.

3 Draw a rectangle for the body, and add legs.

you can do it!

Use a black felt-tip marker for the lines and add color using watercolor paint.

4 Add the arm holding a spear.

5 Draw in a belt and a scabbard.

Splat-a-fact!

Important knights lived in castles.

4

Eagleford Castle

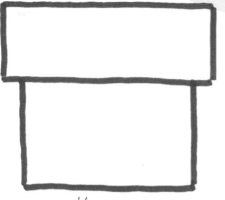

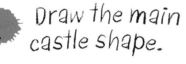

1 Draw the main castle shape.

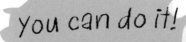

2 Draw in two lines and add the gateway.

you can do it!

Use a blue felt-tip marker for the lines and add color using pencils.

3 Draw in the ramparts.

4 Add a drawbridge and portcullis.

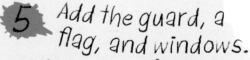

5 Add the guard, a flag, and windows.

splat-a-fact!

The moat and drawbridge kept the castle safe from enemies.

Norman knight

1 Start with the shield.

2 Add the tunic.

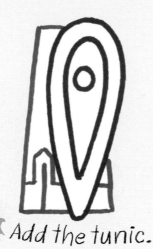

3 Draw in the head with a mouth and a dot for the eye. Add a pointed helmet.

Splat-a-fact!

Norman knights won the Battle of Hastings in 1066.

you can do it!

Use crayons for the color and a black felt-tip marker for the lines.

4 Draw in an arm holding a sword.

5 Add the legs.

Axe knight

1 Cut out a helmet. Draw a slit and breathing holes. Glue down onto colored paper.

2 Cut out a tunic from white paper. Glue down.

3 Now tear out the shield shape and glue down. Tear out a red cross and add to the shield.

splat-a-fact!

Knights could fight with an axe or just throw it at the enemy.

you can do it!

Cut out the knight's armor shapes from tin foil. Use a marker for the details.

4 Cut out legs. Glue down. Add detail.

5 Cut out an arm and the axe head. Cut out the handle. Glue down. Add details.

MAKE SURE YOU GET AN ADULT TO HELP YOU WHEN USING SCISSORS!

10

Archer

1 Start with the head. Add a helmet, a mouth, and a dot for the eye.

2 Add the body and arms.

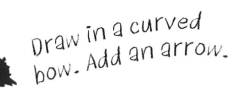

3 Draw in a curved bow. Add an arrow.

4 Add a quiver and belt.

5 Draw in the legs and feet. Finish details.

you can do it!

Use crayons for all textures and paint over with watercolors. Sponge on some of the inks to create added interest.

Ravenswood Castle

1 Start with a square and add a gateway.

2 Draw in the towers and add windows.

you can do it!

Use a soft pencil for the lines and add color using watercolor paint.

splat-a-fact!

The main gate was very strong. It was a thick, iron-studded, wooden door.

3 Draw in triangles for the pointed roofs.

4 Add finishing details: windows, doors, and battlements.

Jousting tent

1 Start with the tent top. Add a wavy line.

2 Draw in the tent with a gap for the entrance.

you can do it!

Use a black felt-tip marker for the lines and add color using colored felt-tip markers.

3 Add stripes and a flag.

splat-a-fact!

The knight's jousting tent was where he got ready for the tournament.

4 Draw the knight's colors on the flag and banner.

16

Jousting knight

1 Start with the horse's head and body.

you can do it!
Use crayons for all textures and paint over with watercolor paint. Use a pencil for the lines.

2 Add the eyes, nostrils, and hooves.

3 Draw in the knight with a helmet. Add his legs on either side of the horse.

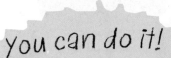

4 Add a lance and shield. Draw feathers on the helmet.

splat-a-fact!
It took about 14 years to train to be a knight.

The joust

1 Start with the horse's head and surcoat.

2 Add its eyes, mouth, tail, and hooves.

you can do it!
Use a brown felt-tip marker for the lines and add color with colored felt-tip markers.

3 Draw in the knight with a shield.

4 Draw in the reins and a saddle. Add detail to the surcoat.

5 Add a lance. Add a feather on the helmet.

splat-a-fact!
A knight needed lots of money—a shiny suit of armor was very expensive.

Mace knight

1 Start with the helmet shape. Add a visor with dots for breathing holes and two slits for the eyes.

2 Add the knight's tunic and shield.

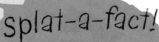

splat-a-fact!

A knight wore his "colors" on his tunic and shield to show who was inside the suit of armor.

3 Add a belt and the legs.

4 Draw in the arm holding a mace.

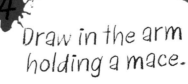

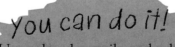

you can do it!

Use colored pencils and a black felt-tip marker for the lines. Smudge or blend the color for more interest.

Hawkbury Castle

1 Cut out the middle section of the castle. Glue down.

2 Cut out two towers. Glue down.

you can do it!

Cut out the shapes from colored paper. Glue these onto a sheet of blue paper. Use felt-tip markers for the lines.

3 Draw in windows and a doorway.

4 Add a guard and a large banner on top.

24

MAKE SURE YOU GET AN ADULT TO HELP YOU WHEN USING SCISSORS!

splat-a-fact!
The walls of a castle were very high to stop attackers from climbing in.

25

Arabian knight

1 Start with the tunic and a round shield. Add details.

2 Add the head, with dots for the eyes, a nose, and a moustache.

3 Add the helmet shape.

you can do it!
Use crayons to create textures and paint over with watercolor paint. Use a soft pencil for the lines.

4 Draw in an arm holding a curved sword.

5 Add the scabbard. Draw in the legs.

Spearman

1 Start with the helmet and the head. Add dots for the eyes and a mouth.

2 Add the tunic.

3 Draw in the arm and spear.

you can do it!

Use a brown felt-tip marker for the lines and add color with soft, chalky pastels. Smudge and blend some of the colors to add interest.

splat-a-fact!

In battle, the spearman could keep enemies at a safe distance with his long spear.

4 Add a long shield shape.

5 Draw in the legs.

Battling knight

1 Start with the helmet. Add slits for the eyes and a pointed beak shape.

you can do it!

Use crayons for texture and paint over it with watercolor paint. Use a felt-tip marker for the lines.

2 Add a shield with a cross.

 3 Draw in a belted tunic with a cross on it.

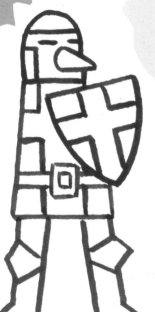 

4 Draw in the legs wearing armor.

5 Add an arm holding a sword overhead.

splat-a-fact!

A knight's suit of armor
had to be built to fit
him exactly.

Index

A
Arabian 26, 27
archer 12, 13
axe 10, 11

B
banner 16, 24
battlements 12, 14
Battle of Hastings, The 8

C
castle 4, 6, 7, 14, 24, 25
crayons 8, 12, 18, 26,
  30

D
drawbridge 6, 7

F
felt-tip marker 4, 6, 8, 16,
  20, 22, 24, 28, 30
flag 6, 16

G
gateway 6, 14
guard 4, 6, 24

H
helmet 4, 8, 10, 12, 18, 20,
22, 26, 28, 30
horse 18–21

J
jousting 16, 18–21

M
mace 22, 23

N
Norman 8

P
pastels 28
pencil 6, 14, 18, 22, 26

S
scabbard 4, 26

shield 4, 8, 10, 12, 18, 20,
  22, 26, 28, 30
spear 4, 28, 29
surcoat 20, 21
sword 8, 26, 27, 30, 31

T
tower 14, 24
tunic 8, 10, 22, 26, 28, 30

W
watercolor 4, 12, 14, 18,
  26, 30